SEVEN SHORTER PLAYS

Seven Shorter Plays

by
CRANE JOHNSON

THEATRE PRESS
550 Fifth Avenue
New York 36, New York

FOR

CATHY, KAREN, SUE

AND JUDY

SEVEN SHORTER PLAYS
Copyright 1966, by
CRANE JOHNSON

All Rights Reserved

Library of Congress Catalog Card No. 66-24283

PRINTED IN THE UNITED STATES OF AMERICA BY
Theo. Gaus' Sons, Inc., BROOKLYN 1, N. Y.

CONTENTS

WAITING

WAITING

MADAME, an older woman
FRANÇOIS, an older girl
FRANCIS, a boy

Setting: Pigalle, Paris
Time: The present or the past

WAITING

(The setting is steps in front of a black curtain which is closed but parted slightly in the middle. When lights are raised there is revealed François, who is painted and dressed as a young girl. She sits on steps looking blankly in front of her. After a moment Madame Blau approaches with Francis. Madame Blau is a buxom, hard-faced woman in her fifties. Francis is a youth in his teens).

MADAME: *(To François)* This is Francis. *(François looks up at him without display of great interest and motions for him to sit beside her, which he does. Madame Blau leaves. Francis looks at her for a moment and then looks out blankly also. After a moment he turns to François and speaks softly to her)*

FRANCIS: What's your name? *(François looks at Francis for a moment, then looks out again)*

FRANÇOIS: *(Matter-of-factly)* Does it matter? *(Francis looks at her and then looks out again. Both look out. Then François speaks without looking at Francis)*

FRANÇOIS: Do you like . . . François? *(Francis doesn't look at François)*

FRANCIS: Very much.

FRANÇOIS: Then call me that. *(Both continue to look out)*

FRANCIS: The regular boy is sick.

FRANÇOIS: Hah! That's his story!

FRANCIS: *(Turning to François, attempting to control his eagerness)* You mean he might not be back?

FRANÇOIS: He'll be back when he's been thrown out . . . *(Looking at Francis)* You're a lot younger.

FRANCIS: I'm seventeen.

FRANÇOIS: I'm not! *(Another long pause)* We follow the the dog act. *(Francis looks at François and she motions toward curtain. Francis rises slowly and looks through curtain)*

FRANÇOIS: We are called "Young Love." *(Francis turns*

*away from the curtain and slowly returns and sits near François
—closer this time)*

FRANCIS *(Softly)* I need the money. I hope I'm good enough. . . . It's so strange . . . the quietness of the audience I mean . . . I thought there'd be more noise.

FRANÇOIS: No noise. Each watcher is a performer himself. Each plays the performer's role.

FRANCIS: I hope I am satisfactory.

FRANÇOIS: You are young. That is for contrast.

FRANCIS: I see.

FRANÇOIS: Bordeaux?

FRANCIS: No, Rouen.

FRANÇOIS: Student?

FRANCIS: For awhile.

FRANÇOIS: And now?

FRANCIS: *(After a pause)* This. *(After a pause)* I need this job . . . Could you help me. *(François looks at Francis for a moment)*

FRANÇOIS: Why did you leave Rouen?

FRANCIS: I wanted to be where life is.

FRANÇOIS: *(Motioning to curtains)* There is life . . . *(Turning to Francis)* Are you a poet?

FRANCIS: I once thought so . . . Words should make the spirit soar, but my words do not.

FRANÇOIS: Why did you come here?

FRANCIS: I have no money. *(Simply)* I am hungry. *(There is another pause. Both look out)*

FRANÇOIS: *(Simply)* I hate men.

FRANCIS: *(Simply)* I'm sorry.

FRANÇOIS: I could get another job if I wanted.

FRANCIS: Will you help me?

FRANÇOIS: Why should I?

FRANCIS: Because I need your help.

FRANÇOIS: The other boy, when he returns, will need work also.

FRANCIS: Please help me.

FRANÇOIS: I once went to Rouen. It is a quiet town and

11

there are green fields all around. And Joan of Arc was burned there.

FRANCIS: Yes, Joan of Arc was burned there.

FRANÇOIS: It must be awful to be burned. To be alive and to be burned.

FRANCIS: Please help me. (*There is a pause*)

FRANÇOIS: (*Slowly*) You must fumble as a young boy. That is your part. You must undress me, but not look at me. Then, you must disrobe, turning your back to me. Then . . . then . . . as you make love . . . you must look only into my eyes, and you must be awkward, but gentle, and look only into my eyes. (*François looks ahead still. Francis places his hands tenderly on hers as Madame Blau approaches and nods toward curtain. Both rise and step through curtain as lights on stage dim out*)

END

THE CONTESSA

THE CONTESSA

CHARACTERS

THE CONTESSA
MARCELLO, her son
CONCETTA, her maid
MRS. GASBY, an American from New Jersey

Setting: Rome. A room in home of The Contessa
Time: The present

THE CONTESSA

(The Contessa is sitting in a satin chair as her grandson is looking out the window. The Contessa is in her sixties. Her grandson is in his early twenties. After the curtains have parted, Marcello looks away from the window).

MARCELLO: Her car has arrived.

CONTESSA: A vulgar Cadillac, no doubt.

MARCELLO: No, an English Ford, I believe.

CONTESSA: Oh, Marcello, my child, how your grandmama has slipped in this world. *(Marcello crosses over and kisses the Contessa)*

CONTESSA: What have I to look forward to? Nothing. All that is left to me in this life is a whoring grandson. *(Sighing)* Ring for Concetta, please. *(Marcello walks right and pulls a cord)*

MARCELLO: I'll go down and meet the lady. *(As Marcello exits right, Concetta the maid enters from left)*

CONCETTA: You rang, Contessa?

CONTESSA: The American has arrived. Please bring the tea things as quickly as possible. I do not wish our encounter to be any longer than necessary. *(Concetta begins to leave)*

CONTESSA: Oh, Concetta. *(Concetta turns)* Please bring me my fan off the desk. *(Concetta does so and then leaves left. The Contessa arranges herself in a regal position. Marcello enters with Mrs. Gasby, a smartly-dressed American in her forties)*

MARCELLO: Grandmama, this is Mrs. Harry Gasby, from America. *(The Contessa nods)*

MRS. GASBY: *(Stepping forward)* How do you do, Contessa. It was so good of you to receive me.

CONTESSA: *(Regally)* Do sit down. I've already ordered tea.

MRS. GASBY: That's wonderful as I really don't have much time.

CONTESSA: Oh? (*This comes as a surprise to the Contessa. She begins using her fan and does so occasionally throughout rest of play*)

MRS. GASBY: I suppose being in a rush is one of the American characteristics.

CONTESSA: Yes, unfortunately.

MRS. GASBY: But then, we do get things done, don't we, Contessa?

CONTESSA: I'm afraid I have had little experience with things American.

MRS. GASBY: What a pity! (*Concetta enters with tea things and places them on the table in front of the Contessa. The Contessa begins pouring tea into a cup*)

CONTESSA: Cream or lemon?

MRS. GASBY: (*Sweetly*) Neither. (*The Contessa hands the cup to Concetta, who takes it to Mrs. Gasby. The Contessa nods to Concetta to leave and she does. Mrs. Gasby takes one sip of tea, puts it down and does not pick up the cup again*)

MARCELLO: Mrs. Gasby's husband is in plumbing. New Jersey, I believe.

MRS. GASBY: East Rutherford, to be exact. Harry is most interested in the common market.

CONTESSA: (*Rather chillily*) Interest in things common seems to be the blight of our era.

MARCELLO: Mrs. Gasby's husband is planning to open a branch office here in Rome.

CONTESSA: Then you'll be living here, be part of our little social world.

MRS. GASBY: Only for awhile. Harry and I prefer London and, of course, Paris. We'll be here only as long as necessary.

CONTESSA: But even so you'll want to be properly presented.

MRS. GASBY: Yes, that is why Mrs. Bloomsdale arranged for us to meet.

CONTESSA: Mrs. Bloomsdale and I have been friends since the first World War. The Americans have changed I've noticed.

MRS. GASBY: The world does move on.

17

CONTESSA: A proper introduction to Rome Society is most important.

MRS. GASBY: Oh, indeed.

CONTESSA: One's existence and happiness in Rome depend on it.

MRS. GASBY: You are so right, Contessa.

MARCELLO: Unfortunately, Grandmama, Mrs. Gasby must leave Rome . . . temporarily . . . at the end of the month.

MRS. GASBY: Yes, on September 29.

CONTESSA: Oh, how unfortunate!

MRS. GASBY: Why, dear lady?

CONTESSA: I am at the utter control of my banker and will not have my next quarter's allowance until October 1. I would not dream of presenting you to Rome society unless it could be done properly.

MRS. GASBY: Oh, but you must allow me to help.

CONTESSA: Don't speak of it, dear lady.

MRS. GASBY: I insist! A quiet affair with, say, about a hundred of your friends, with a minimum of ten titles.

CONTESSA: Ten titles?

MRS. GASBY: Perhaps a garden party. A gala with costumes. In your garden. Music and lanterns. (*Goes to window*) Oh dear, the garden needs a great deal of work, doesn't it? Pity! Well, perhaps a ball. (*Looking around*) This room needs redecorating. If we had a ball with just candlelight, perhaps it wouldn't show. Let's see, a ball, for one hundred people, with minimum of ten titles. Dinner, champagne, the orchestra, attendants. (*Sitting again*) How much would that amount to, Contessa?

CONTESSA: (*Thinking quickly*) There are always extras, so it is difficult to be exact.

MRS. GASBY: Approximately, Contessa.

CONTESSA: As you say, much work must be done. I think perhaps about 15,000 lire.

MRS. GASBY: That's $2400.00.

CONTESSA: More or less.

MRS. GASBY: And you'll guarantee ten titles.

18

CONTESSA: Yes.

MRS. GASBY: I think the Saturday before I leave would be most appropriate.

CONTESSA: (*To Marcello*) Bring me my appointment book, will you, Marcello? (*Marcello crosses left to desk and returns with book and hands it to Contessa who flips through pages. Marcello stands behind Contessa*)

CONTESSA: Yes, that will be most satisfactory.

MRS. GASBY: And will your grandson be free that evening? I have a daughter about his age who will be needing an escort.

MARCELLO: I shall be most delighted, Mrs. Gasby.

MRS. GASBY: She has a beau back home—a sophomore at Princeton. We're quite pleased with him, but he won't be able to fly over. So its' *just an escort* we're interested in. Are you titled.

MARCELLO: Yes, Mrs. Gasby, I am titled.

MRS. GASBY: That will look well in the papers.

CONTESSA: The papers. I forgot. And the photographers. That will be extra. About 1,000 lire.

MRS. GASBY: Another $160.00.

CONTESSA: It will be best for me to make the contacts. Actually, some of them are friends of Marcello.

MRS. GASBY: *Indeed?* I've always considered newsmen and their photographers a rather low lot. (*Looking around*) It'd be a pity to change anything here. There's such a charming decadence about it all. The smaller salon I passed through is rather smart.

CONTESA: (*Stiffly*) That is the only room we've done over.

MRS. GASBY: One could entertain there, couldn't one?

CONTESSA: Why, I suppose one could.

MRS. GASBY: For tea, perhaps.

CONTESSA: I suppose for only tea.

MRS. GASBY: How much, Contessa, for afternoon tea with ten titles and your grandson to escort my daughter, and newsmen and photographers.

CONTESSA: Instead of the ball?

MRS. GASBY: Instead of the ball.

19

CONTESSA: About 6,000 lire.

MRS. GASBY: That's about $960.00. (*Rising*) I'm afraid that is a little steep. The Princess Ragsveil will give me a tea with twelve titles, newsmen and photographers for $800.00.

CONTESSA: Princess Ragsveil!

MRS. GASBY: (*Bitchily*) I'm such a dumbell about titles, but isn't a princess higher than a contessa?

CONTESSA: It is the family that matters. (*Mrs. Gasby takes out checkbook and sits in chair*)

MRS. GASBY: Shall we say 700 American dollars. Half now and half upon appearance of the ten titles, newsmen and photographers. (*Contessa looks angrily at Marcello who hesitates a moment and then nods to Contessa*)

CONTESSA: I like the directness you Americans display. Most of the Americans I've known were of the older breed. Innocents who displayed some awe of position and the old titled families.

MRS. GASBY: Time does move on, doesn't it, Contessa?

CONTESSA: Yes, fortunately. I am wondering, Mrs. Gasby, if you could possibly make out the check for the full amount.

MRS. GASBY: $700.00?

CONTESSA: Yes, if it wouldn't be inconvenient.

MRS. GASBY: My husband wouldn't, but I feel I can trust you.

CONTESSA: We are an old family. Our word is as treasure. (*Mrs. Gasby writes out the check, rises and hands it to Contessa who takes it*)

CONTESSA: I'll have *this* room done over, made presentable. And I'll invite the ten titles and others, old friends of good families, and my grandson will escort your daughter, and there will be newsmen and photographers and you will be properly introduced into Rome society. It will be a gracious introduction, with dignity. (*Rising*) And it will be my gift to you, Mrs. Gasby. (*Contessa begins tearing the check into shreds and letting them drop to the floor*)

CONTESSA: Until we meet again, Mrs. Gasby, at your tea. (*Mrs. Gasby is bewildered*)

CONTESSA: Marcello, please escort Mrs. Gasby to the door.
(*Marcello steps right*)
CONTESSA: Goodbye, Mrs. Gasby, until the tea.
MRS. GASBY: There's surely a mistake . . .
CONTESSA: (*Proudly*) A mistake? Whose, Mrs. Gasby?
Whose? (*The Contessa smiles victoriously as Marcello escorts Mrs. Gasby out of the room*)

END

OCCASION

OCCASION

CHARACTER

MISS ANDREWS

Setting: Her apartment
Time: The present

OCCASION

(Miss Mary Andrews, a private secretary in her early forties, enters a tight living room of a second class residential hotel. She is carrying groceries, etc., which she takes into her small kitchenette. A moment later she returns to the living room and begins taking off her hat and coat. These she places on a chair. Then Miss Andrews sits down, kicks off shoes, and lies back relaxed. A moment later Miss Andrews looks around slowly. She then gets up, walks around the room and touches various items. She then goes over to the wall, takes the earphone of her apartment intercommunication unit, and places it to her ear. Mary pushes the buzzer of the unit and soon speaks into the mouthpiece).

MISS ANDREWS: Hello, Mr. Garson? This is Miss Andrews in apartment 416. I was wondering, if by chance, there was a letter for me that you might have overlooked in delivering today. *(Pause)* No letter? I see. Were there any callers? I mean anyone who called but didn't leave names? None? None at all. Thank you, Mr. Garson. *(As after-thought)* It was nice talking to you. *(Miss Andrews puts the earpiece back slowly on the hook, looks about her, then goes slowly into the kitchenette, and brings out a birthday cake which she places on the table center stage. She then lights the candles and sits at left side of table watching the burning candles. After a moment she begins singing softly)*

MISS ANDREWS: *(Singing)* Happy Birthday to Me,
Happy Birthday to Me,
Happy Birthday, Dear Mary,
Happy Birthday to Me.

(Miss Andrews look at the cake for a moment more, then buries her head in arms and begins to cry as curtains close)

THE END

REMEMBRANCE

REMEMBRANCE

CHARACTERS

PAUL CAILLOT, a bachelor in his thirties
MME. RAMIEUX, a married woman in her forties

Setting: Caillot's studio in Paris
Time: The past

REMEMBRANCE

(The scene is the studio of Paul Caillot. When the scene opens Caillot is playing at his harpsicord, making notations on the musical score frequently as he plays and composes. After a moment there is a knock at the door right. Caillot continues playing. Again there is the knocking).

CAILLOT: Entrez. (*Mme. Raimeux enters—a beautiful woman in her forties. When Paul sees her, he motions her to a chair. Mme Raimeux is indignant, but seats herself. After a moment Paul stops his playing but does not look at Mme Raimeux*)

MME RAIMEUX: (*Indignantly*) Monsieur Caillot, I came only to tell you in person what an arrogant, detestable person I think you are. (*Paul does not look at her but makes a notation with pencil on his score*)

MME RAMIEUX: (*Continuing*) I am not like the other women in Paris, available at your slightest bidding. The idea! A formal reception. Our first meeting. And I, the wife of France's leading industrialist. Such affrontry! To invite me here at this hour. A formal reception. Our first meeting. I, a married woman. A woman of honor and respect. A woman whose reputation is untarnished. Oh, I've heard of your successes! All Paris has. Even the details are known! Oh, the affrontry! The insult! I have come only to let you know there is one woman in France who is impervious to your seemingly insatiable desires. (*Paul still doesn't look at her, but makes a notation with pencil on his score*)

MME RAMIEUX: (*Rising*) I am leaving. Still a woman of respect. (*Goes to door, but turns*) Have you nothing to say?

CAILLOT: (*Indicating*) The screen is over there. (*Mme Raimeux pauses at the door*)

MME RAMIEUX: (*Softly, with horror*) It's true. Every word. A beast. Only a beast.

CAILOT: (*Softly*) True. Every word. True.

MME RAMIEUX: A formal reception. Our first meeting. Your impossible invitation.

CAILLOT. You are here.

MME RAMIEUX: Only to let you know the impossibility of your proposal.

CAILLOT: (*After pause*) Leave, if you like.

MME RAMIEUX: Why would I stay.

CAILLOT: No reason, really.

MME RAMIEUX: No reason.

CAILLOT: My invitation to you had one intent only.

MME RAMIEUX: Beast!

CAILLOT: You are the wife of our country's leading industrialist. That is true. A woman of honor and respect. A woman whose reputation is untarnished. All true. True. That is how all Paris views you. But not how I view you. (*Mme Ramieux holds her breath slightly*) I view you only as a desirable woman to lure into my bed.

MME RAMIEUX: At a formal reception. Our first meeting. I have a soul. You might have been interested in that.

CAILLOT: Your soul does not interest me.

MME RAMIEUX: You have probably never before met a woman of such great respectability.

CAILLOT: That is true.

MME RAMIEUX: And your only desire is to bring about my ruin.

CAILLOT: My only desire is to bed you.

MME RAMIEUX: You are mad.

CAILLOT: Leave if you like.

MME RAMIEUX: All Paris knows of your reputation.

CAILLOT: That I can have anyone I want . . . (*Turning directly to her*) You are ten years older than I . . . Even your husband would be proud to hear I desired you.

MME RAMIEUX: He knows. (*Stepping left*) All Paris knows. (*Caillot turns away and begins playing softly again*)

MME RAMIEUX: Men hired by my husband followed me here. If I should remain a moment longer it will be all over

31

Paris that I have become your lover. That a woman ten years older has become your mistress. (*Caillot continues his playing*)

MME RAMIEUX: (*Plaintively*) Do you truly desire me?

CAILLOT: (*Simply*) I am a man.

MME RAMIEUX: My soul, truly I have a beautiful soul . . . (*Caillot waves a hand toward her in annoyance*)

MME RAMIEUX: (*Turning right and speaking almost to herself*) I am lost. (*Caillot stops his playing*)

CAILLOT: In forty years you will be eighty. I shall be dead. Composers die young. And when you are eighty, what will you have to tell—to think about? What will they whisper about behind your back when you are eighty years old? One thing. That when you were forty you were seduced—by Paul Caillot, the composer who was thirty years old and had his pick of Paris . . . (*Spoken softly, after a pause*) Go, my dear, if you must.

MME RAMIEUX: (*Very softly*) You would not send me away.

CAILLOT: I am a cruel man. Brutal. A beast.

MME RAMIEUX: (*Softly*) You would not send me away. (*Caillot softly folds his hands in his lap and looks directly at Mme Ramieux*)

CALLOT: What will you tell people when you are eighty.

MME RAMIEUX: (*Turning to him hypnotically*) That I was seduced by a man ten years younger. A man who had no interest in my soul. A man consumed in desire . . . Desire for me.

CAILLOT: (*Softly, pathetically*) I am a cruel man. A brutal man.

MME RAMIEUX: (*With great feeling*) You are Paul Caillot! (*They look at each other for a moment, then Mme Ramieux goes toward the screen as Paul Caillot commences his playing again and the curtains close*)

END

SCENE

SCENE

FRANK
KENNY
BERNADETTE

Setting: A room in a bachelor apartment
Time: The present

SCENE

(As the scene opens, Kenny, a young man in his mid-twenties, stands in front of a mirror putting on his tie. He addresses his remarks to someone in adjoining room).

KENNY: Still wish you'd change your mind and go with us, Frank. Just think, one poor little ole extra girl with no one but Kenny Boy to take care of her.

FRANK: *(Offstage voice)* Only *one* extra should prove no problem for you, Kenny. *(Frank, a man in his late twenties, enters in his stocking feet and carries a tie. He walks over to behind Kenny and looks over Kenny's shoulder into the mirror as he fixes his tie)* I'm meeting Bernadette at nine. To go look at drapery materials.

KENNY: Real lively evening. How's the house coming?

FRANK: Fine.

KENNY: And your trip. Still Bermuda?

FRANK: Yeah, that's not much of a honeymoon. Two weeks in Bermuda, but the house is costing us a lot more than we'd planned. *(Frank goes over to sofa chair right, sits, and begins putting on his shoes which are nearby)*

KENNY: You're both very lucky people. You and this Bernadette. *(Brushing his hair)* That's what we all want. A nice decent girl. To love, and to marry, and to setle down.

FRANK: Can't see you ever settling down.

KENNY: If I could meet just one nice girl.

FRANK: There're lots of nice girls, Kenny. All around. Just be nice yourself and you'll meet them.

KENNY: Just be nice, he says. I try to, Frank, but happens? I go into action. Knock 'em off. Don't mean to, don't even try half the time. Just reflex action. *(Frank laughs)*

KENNY: And I hate myself afterwards. Cause it was all so easy. And cause it means nothing to me. Nothing at all.

FRANK: I pity you, Kenny, I really do.

KENNY: Go on, it's not that bad.

FRANK: Being so compulsive about sex. Lining 'em up and knockin' 'em down. Just like an animal. Where's the fun?

KENNY: No fun at all. (*Frank rises, puts on coat, and goes to door*)

FRANK: Well, best of luck tonight, Kenny, with both of them. But you're the last guy I know who needs the luck! (*Frank laughs and leaves. Kenny goes into bedroom area and returns with coat which he puts on. He then again looks into mirror and brushes his hair. The telephone rings*)

KENNY: Hello . . . What? Well, why can't she come to the phone herself? Where are you? Let me talk to Nancy; I'm pretty damned unhappy about this . . . Hello . . . Hello . . . (*Kenny in disbelief hangs up phone, then becomes a little angry. He goes to mirror and with his hand, messes up his hair. The doorbell of the apartment rings. He is surprised, but hopeful. He attempts to smooth his hair with his hands as he crosses right to doorway. He soon reappears with Bernadette. Bernadette is an Italian type, clean-cut girl in her early twenties*)

KENNY: So you're Frank's girl.

BERNADETTE: Fiancée.

KENNY: Well, I can understand now why he never brought you around!

BERNADETTE: I got off work a little early and just took a chance Frank might still be here. I won't bother you, Mr. . . . (*Bernadette turns to leave*)

KENNY: The name is Kenny. But don't rush off. Stay for one drink.

BERNADETTE: I really mustn't.

KENNY: That's not being very hospitable. Here I am, Frank's roommate, his best friend, and you won't even stay for one drink to toast my pal's forthcoming marriage.

BERNADETTE: (*Smiling*) You've shamed me into it. (*Sitting on sofa*) But only one. (*Kenny goes over to bureau and takes out liquor and then goes to refrigerator and takes out bowl of cubes and drops some into glasses. He doesn't turn toward Bernadette as he gives his next speech*)

37

KENNY: You work for some sort of agency, don't you?

BERNADETTE: Scripts.

KENNY *(Turning)* Scene! *(Acting it out)* Nice young girl comes to pick up her affianced. To go out drape buying. He is gone. But in the apartment is his roommate. A rat. *(Aside)* I am a rat, you know that, don't you, Bernadette.

BERNADETTE: So I've been informed.

KENNY: *(Play-acting)* A compulsive sexual maniac. Guided only by his animal instincts. *Question*: Will the rat attempt to make the fiancée of his best friend on the evening of their wedding? Tune in tomorrow, dear friends. *(Hands drink to Bernadette)* I can't get over it. A girl like you, a knock-out, and a guy like Frank gets you.

BERNADETTE: He's a fine man; he'll make a wonderful father.

KENNY: *(Directly)* Is that all you Catholic girls want in a man, a wonderful father?

BERNADETTE: Why, no . . .

KENNY: Don't you care . . . or want a man who can make love? *(Bernadette puts down her drink and rises)*

KENNY: *(Acting)* Wait! Don't turn that knob! Will the rat continue in this vein. Will there be any sense of decency rising in him to turn him off his course. He has known so few nice girls. All have yielded. To his charm. To his approach. To his sense of knowing the right approach in every situation. He's a rat, friends of the audience. He knows it. The girl knows it. But he's a man and the girl is doomed to a "nice" boy who'll make a good husband, impregnating her dutifully at the recommended intervals. *(Bernadette turns from Kenny. He goes to her)*

KENNY: Look at me, Bernadette. Frank bores you stiff. Admit it. You'd swap him in a moment if a real man came along.

BERNADETTE: *(Turning to him)* Your imagination is exceeded only by your vulgarity. *(Bernadette starts right. Kenny crosses in her path)*

KENNY: *Scene!* The nice young girl attempts to leave as she properly should. But the rat jumps in her path. Out of habit he wishes to ruin her. *(Directly)* Go on, marry the jerk. But aren't you entitled, isn't every girl entitled to one terrific experience before she settles down to . . . (*Bernadette begins crossing again. As she attempts to go around Kenny, he grabs her by the wrist*)

KENNY: *Scene!* Violence. Will the rat rape her!

BERNADETTE: Please, you're hurting me.

KENNY: Please, please, please. You'll like it and I need it so.

BERNADETTE: (*Struggling*) I'll scream . . . (*Kenny quickly cups his hand across her mouth as he locks her to him with the same arm*)

KENNY: (*Feverishly*) Just once you'll see what a man is like. You'll love it, baby, I promise. Oh baby, baby. (*With his free hand, Kenny begins ripping Bernadette's blouse*)

KENNY: And you want me. You want me. I sense it. You want me to take you. You want it, you want it. (*Bernadette breaks away from Kenny and steps right. Kenny takes a step toward Bernadette who turns and slaps him hard across the face. Kenny stands stunned for a moment before speaking*)

KENNY: I want you. Very much . . . (*Bernadette grabs her purse off chair and turns to Kenny. She attempts to think of something vile enough to say, but can't, so she looks at him a moment and then leaves. Kenny stands for a moment stunned, then takes out address book and walks toward the phone*)

KENNY: *Scene!* The nice girl has escaped. The rat takes out his telephone book. He walks to the phone (*Which he does*) He looks through it for a number. (*Which he does*) He begins dialing. (*Which he does*) But before completing his call, he stops and lets the receiver hang loosely in his hand. (*Which he does*) Cold. Empty. His just dessert. Rejected. Unwanted. (*Slowly the door opens and Bernadette enters and just stands. Kenny turns slowly and looks at her as the lights dim slowly out*)

THE END

39

THE MAD PROFESSOR

THE MAD PROFESSOR

CHARACTERS

THE PROFESSOR
THE COLLEAGUE
THE WAITER

Setting: A room in a restaurant
Time: The present or the past

THE MAD PROFESSOR

(The scene is a table in a restaurant. The two men are sitting at the table).

COLLEAGUE: But, my dear colleague, how is it possible, if you are mad as you say, that you are able to continue at the university where one of the regulations specifically prohibits the continuance in employment of professors who have become mad. *(The Professor is about to answer when the Waiter enters with chocolate which he places before the two men. The Waiter leaves)*

PROFESSOR: Very simple. I myself noticed that some of my actions seemed irrational. So I made a thorough study of my behavior.

COLLEAGUE: *(Repeating)* You made a thorough study of your behavior.

PROFESSOR: Yes, using all my training in logic, I was forced to come to the conclusion that I was mad. Quite mad.

COLLEAGUE: *(Repeating)* Quite mad.

PROFESSOR: Thus, since logic could no longer be an ally, I forsook it and was forced to turn to cleverness.

COLLEAGUE: Cleverness. And what did you do, Professor?

PROFESSOR: I immediately confided in certain members of my department that I was mad. There are in every department those who immediately spread every bit of news and gossip and rumor to other members of the department. To these I confided that I was mad.

COLLEAGUE: That you were mad.

PROFESSOR: Yes, and then, as an extra measure, I did things that only a mad man would do. I did these purposely.

COLLEAGUE: Not because you were mad, but because you wanted them to think you were mad.

PROFESSOR: That is correct.

COLLEAGUE: And whispering to everyone that you *were* mad.

PROFESSOR: That is correct.

COLLEAGUE: And because you told everyone you were mad when the question arose as to your madness the only response was laughter.

PROFESSOR: The only response was laughter.

COLLEAGUE: So there would be no investigation regarding your madness.

PROFESSOR: Madness.

COLLEAGUE: How clever! A madman could not be so clever.

PROFESSOR: Wrong! A mad man can be very clever.

COLLEAGUE: I do not believe that you are mad.

PROFESSOR: But I am.

COLLEAGUE: We will talk no more on the topic. This is simply a humor.

PROFESSOR: I *am* mad. I admit it. All the evidence testifies to it.

COLLEAGUE: A humor simply. And besides, one cannot be contentedly mad unless one has a private income.

PROFESSOR: I have a private income. Rather large.

COLLEAGUE: My wife and I are entertaining Saturday night. Will you honor us with your presence.

PROFESSOR: Of course.

COLLEAGUE: More chocolate? (*The Professor nods and the Colleague pours more chocolate as the lights dim*)

END

THE DRY CLEANER'S BOY

THE DRY CLEANER'S BOY

CHARACTERS

JIM, a white boy
GEORGE, his lover

Setting: Jim's apartment in Atlanta
Time: The present

THE DRY CLEANER'S BOY

(The scene opens on living room of Jim's two room apartment in Atlanta. Jim, a white boy in his middle twenties, sits at table center sipping coffee and glancing at a newspaper he has in front of him. He wears shirt, tie, etc., but no coat).

JIM: *(Glancing at watch)* Hey, George, you'll be late for the office *(There is the sound of an electric razor off-stage left)*

GEORGE: *(His voice coming from offstage left)* Three minutes more.

JIM: *(After pause)* Thanks, George, for last night.

GEORGE: *(Over noise of razor)* And thank you, Jim.

JIM: You were pretty wonderful, you know.

GEORGE: Not bad yourself.

JIM: Did I hurt you, George?

GEORGE: Why do you ask?

JIM: You were pretty tight.

GEORGE: Don't do *that* very often. *(Jim takes another sip of coffee and looks at paper)*

JIM: Will you come here again, George?

GEORGE: If you want me to.

JIM: I want you to. *(Pause)* George, did you work out with weights.

GEORGE: A couple years ago. Should I start again?

JIM: No, you're just right. *(Pause)* George, should I work out with weights?

GEORGE: No, I like you as you are.

JIM: You slept last night didn't you?

GEORGE: A little.

JIM: I didn't.

GEORGE: I'm sorry.

JIM: You excite me too much.

GEORGE: That will pass.

JIM: Think so?

GEORGE: And then you won't want me coming again.

JIM: Never happen.

GEORGE: I like coming here, Jim. I want to come even after we're tired of sex with one another. Jim, what are your interests? Art?

JIM: I know the terminology but have no feeling.

GEORGE: Theatre?

JIM: Don't understand it.

GEORGE: Music?

JIM: Yes.

GEORGE: Hayden?

JIM: Very much.

GEORGE: I have records. I'll bring them. We'll play them and I'll cook for you, Jim.

JIM: I like plain food, but subtly spiced.

GEORGE: My grandmother taught me how to use spices (*Jim looks at his watch*)

JIM: George, you'll be late for the office.

GEORGE: On my way now. (*George steps through entrance-way. He is a Negro in his early twenties and is stripped to the waist. He puts on his shirt*)

JIM: (*Good-naturedly*) For Christ's sake, George, put on your shirt before I drag you off to bed again.

GEORGE: (*Teasing*) I'd like that.

JIM: And we'd both lose our jobs for being late. No thanks. (*Jim gets up and puts on his coat. George quickly puts on tie and his coat and they start for the door right*)

JIM: George, can you make it Tuesday.

GEORGE: After work? After dark? (*Jim nods*)

GEORGE: Yes, I can make it. (*Jim turns to door*)

GEORGE: Jim.

JIM: Yes.

GEORGE: I came in the dark. It's light now. Nine o'clock in the morning. Morning in a large apartment house. Morning in Atlanta. (*Jim understands. He crosses left over to closet and takes out a pair of pants. He hands them to George*)

JIM: (*Gaily*) You're the Dry Cleaner's Boy. (*George walks left and stands behind Jim*)

GEORGE: Who walks three feet behind. (*George measures the three feet and stands behind Jim. Jim starts toward door, but turns, goes to George, spreads his arms apart, and embraces and kisses him. He then turns, measures the three feet, walks and turns*)

JIM: Tuesday?

GEORGE: Tuesday. (*Jim winks at George. George winks back and they exit, George being careful to remain three feet behind Jim*)

END

DATE DUE

DEC 12 '72			
JAN 9 '74			
FEB 1 '75			
APR 29 76			
MAY 10 '76			
APR 9 72			
APR 15 '80			
APR 16 '81			
APR 4 '88			
MAY 10 '89			
JUL 8 96			
JUL 15 '96			
SEP 28 '96			
MAR 11 '03			